Find Out About Farming

by Helen Gregory

Consultant:
Adria F. Klein, Ph.D.
California State University, San Bernardino

capstone classroom
Heinemann Raintree • Red Brick Learning
division of Capstone

There are many different types of farms.
Some farms have acres of wheat blowing in the summer breeze.

A rice farm might have many paddies.
A paddy is a wet field.
The rice grows on long stems that look like grass.

Some farms grow fruit.

This farm grows oranges. These rows of trees are called an orange grove.

Some farms are big.
This farm grows many
different types of crops.

Some farms are small.
This farm grows tomatoes.

Some farms need very hot weather. Pineapples only grow where it is hot.

Banana farms need hot weather, too. This banana farm is in the rain forest.

Some farms need cool weather. Pumpkins grow best where it is cool.

An apple farm needs cool weather too.

Some farms have livestock. Animals are an important part of this farm.

Dairy farms raise cows. Cows give milk.

Poultry farms raise chickens and turkeys. Chickens lay eggs.

Mixed farms are where animals and crops are both important to the farmer.

Some farms are called hobby farms.
These are farms people have just for fun.